The Painted Desert

Gregory McNamee, SERIES EDITOR

# The Painted Desert

## Land of Wind and Stone

TEXT BY Scott Thybony

PHOTOGRAPHS BY David Edwards

The University of Arizona Press    Tucson

The University of Arizona Press
Text © 2006 Scott Thybony
Photographs © 2006 David Edwards
All rights reserved

♾ This book is printed on acid-free, archival-quality paper.
Manufactured in the United States of America

11  10  09  08  07  06    6  5  4  3  2  1

Library of Congress Cataloging-in-Publication Data appear on
the last printed page of this book.

Frontispiece: Rockscape, Ward Terrace

contents

CONTENTS

viii

# photographs

# The Painted Desert

# introduction

Trees fall away as the highway leaves the mountains, thinning to a scatter of junipers. Soon nothing remains for the eye to settle on but the roll of grasslands and a far-reaching sky that curves down to the Painted Desert. A faint line of cliffs marks a horizon so far away I recognize it only from memory. But that's enough.

Spanish explorers called the region where I'm going El Desierto Pintado, a name revived in its English form three centuries later. Cross the badlands when the light separates at the end of day, and the choice of names becomes obvious. The landscape turns prismatic in a flare-up of color—what I always thought were countless hues. But Americans will run the numbers given half a chance, and some enthusiasts have managed to identify 168 distinct colors and shades.

Pressed between the Little Colorado River on the south and bold escarpments on the north, the Painted Desert curves for roughly 200 miles across northeastern Arizona from near the Zuni River to the Colorado. Much of the wind-carved expanse lies within the Navajo Indian country, and forms the geographic tissue connecting Petrified Forest National Park with Grand Canyon National Park.

To reach it, photographer Dave Edwards and I follow Highway 89, running north from the San Francisco Peaks to the reservation town of Cameron. We are taking two trucks as insurance in case the weather turns or the mood hits us to head off in separate directions. We bring food, water, and spare gas to last four days—enough time to cross what for me is the heart of the desert. Our route will follow a forty-mile sweep of cliffs, running roughly north and south, between the Hopi mesas and the ancient ruins of Wupatki.

It's a region lying beyond the river where the roads fade into a narrative landscape. Each butte is a remnant of an older story, half remembered, worn to fragments. Where we're heading, the present thinly coats the past the way living dunes drift across bedrock. That's the way I'll tell it, letting my memories of the place become part of the story wherever they outcrop.

Already the drive through familiar country north of the peaks has released a flicker of images. Roads branch off where I've been stuck in the mud and buried in snow drifts. I know which volcanic cones were swept by wildfire, and where the elk gather in the fall. I remember Basque sheepherders trailing their herds past the homestead where we lived, and cowboys from the CO Bar Ranch driving cattle to winter range. I recognize the places where Navajo medicine men pray for rain and where Hopi priests leave prayer feathers. I recall reading Zane Grey's account of traveling horseback through here on his first encounter with the mythic West, and saw the myth reshaped when Captain America pulled into the Sacred Mountain Trading Post in a scene from *Easy Rider.*

For a number of years, I lived in a remote homestead without electricity and heated by wood. Water had to be hauled thirty miles from town, the last eight up a dirt road to Indian Flat. In winter our nearest neighbors lived at the trading post nine miles away. While living at the ranch, I first began to explore the Painted Desert. Each evening when I returned from town, the desert would appear far to the north, a band of light shimmering along the horizon like a mirage, more a place of the imagination than solid geography.

Images overlap in crossbedded layers along the highway, and beneath them lies the dark and tangible history of an older frontier. Kick the ground, and traces of bone and ash surface. The road passes the burned walls of Medicine Fort and the violent scenes sealed below Deadman Flat. Villages laid to waste and abandoned forever, victims left where they fell to be buried by drift sand. Some turn away from the hard past. On this trip I'll go deeper into it, so far back in time the bones themselves have turned to stone.

The highway sheds 3,000 feet of elevation as we pass from winter into spring, from mountain green to the Triassic reds of shale and siltstone. Soon the two of us pull into the Cameron Trading Post, a cluster of stone buildings above the Little Colorado River and a bridge length away from the actual desert. It's the main event for a hundred miles, and judging by the crowded parking lot, few travelers can resist it. Tour buses, trucks pulling boats down from Lake Powell, rental cars returning from the Grand Canyon, and pickups in from the sheep camps all end up here.

Dave and I are no different. We leave the trucks to stretch our legs and pass some fossil tracks preserved in a flagstone walkway. The ancient reptile had an oversize pinkie resembling a thumb. This led early investigators to guess, wrongly it turned out, that *Cheirotherium* walked in a cross-legged stagger, a trait I've always associated with our own species. Inside the trading post, we become separated in the thicket of trinkets and the press of bodies. A woman dodges past a rack of scorpions and tarantulas encased in globs of acrylic resin and makes a beeline for the jewelry. I overhear her telling a friend, "I want to find something that enhances my self-worth." The old quest.

At the back of the store, a clerk spreads out a new Navajo rug that sells for $325. If you prefer an old weaving from the 1820s, they have that too, but it will cost you a thousand times as much. Past the rugs, I reach the restaurant, where a man sits alone at a table digging into a Navajo taco with its layers of beans, meat, and lettuce piled on a piece of Indian fry bread the size of a hubcap. The menu also offers Navajo stew without the mutton, which is like serving clam chowder without the mollusk. I fill up a Styrofoam cup with coffee and leave it at that.

Outside, an older Navajo sits next to the yellow "Your Wate and Fate" scale, entertained by the ebb and flow of tourists. He watches a boy return to the family SUV, sent by his father to retrieve something inside. Leaving the car, the boy shuts the door and immediately realizes his mistake. He runs back to the store, and his father marches out, angrily circling the car and testing every door. The boy has locked the keys inside with the headlights on. The mother stands back, holding her son's hand. "Just stay away!" the father orders, "Just keep him away!"

I hear the Navajo comment under his breath, "Should have gone back to the car himself."

We need to get moving. A two-lane bridge carries traffic above the bed of the river, which is sunk a hundred feet below. Out of habit, I glance down to see if it's flowing. Barely a trickle braids across the sands, a good sign. In the days ahead we'll be taking the back roads or no roads at all, so a little moisture will make the sand easier to cross.

Early exploring parties called the river the Río Colorado Chiquito, and over time it became the Little Colorado River, one of those Spanish-English splices so common in the Southwest. The river drains an immense 26,000 square miles of Arizona and New Mexico, but the bed is often mud cracked and dust dry, a clue to the arid character of the region. The headwaters of the Little Colorado rise high in the White Mountains, and during spring runoff the melting snows turn it into a real river for a couple of weeks. It soon runs dry again, until floods flash through it in pulses during the summer rains. At those times the floodwaters churn beneath the bridge, and before reaching the main Colorado, descend through a gorge cut 3,000 feet deep in less than sixty miles.

Motorists who cross over the bridge at highway speeds rarely notice the river below, but crossings were once taken more seriously. When I scouted this part of the Navajo reservation with tribal ranger Jim Tom, he talked about the four sacred rivers that formed the boundaries of his ancestral homeland: the Rio Grande to the east, the Little Colorado on the south, the Colorado to the west, and the San Juan on the north. In the old days, he said, before the Navajo made a crossing they prayed for safety and success on their journey. Offerings of pollen, turquoise, shell, and jet were placed on the bank. These could not be tossed in the river but had to be left where the water, as it lapped the sand, could take them at the proper time. He didn't say what they did when it was dry.

In a split second I'm across the bridge and into the Painted Desert. Dave follows and we turn onto a dirt track, entering a corner of the desert best known to a few sheepherders and geologists. Of the two, I'd rather be making my living out here from rocks rather than grass. It's barren terrain, where a scattering of plants appears to have fallen from the sky rather than sprouted from the ground. Scientists classify it as a cold desert, lying above 4,000 feet in elevation. Temperatures often fall below freezing in winter, and snowstorms sweep across it. But the heat can be brutal at midday in summer, and you often find yourself searching for a piece of shade even in a cold desert.

Sentinels below Adeii Eechii Cliffs

A few homesteads lie near an abandoned stretch of the old highway as forgotten as the landscape. The unpaved road we take follows a dirt airstrip past what we call the Field of Dreams, a rusted backstop in an empty desert. Broken beer bottles begin to thin out and fragments of petrified wood increase, as we move beyond town. Tire tracks branch off, and I follow them toward a breach in the first line of cliffs, a step between the river-carved terraces. Climbing, we punch through a sand dune anchored in place by clumps of narrowleaf yucca and ascend the margin of an arroyo, treacherous in wet weather. At the top of the escarpment, the track disappears into the stark expanse of the Ward Terrace.

## a lost landscape

Most people only know the Painted Desert from having pulled off at the Petrified Forest National Park exit on Interstate 40. If they happen to hit it at midday, as most do, they'll find a landscape drained of color and flattened under the direct sunlight. A snapshot, and they're off to Meteor Crater.

"The next stop is Petrified Crater," I once heard a woman tell her husband as they prepared to leave. "No," he corrected her, "it's Petrified Meteor."

Early travelers had a far different experience. Zane Grey's encounter with the Painted Desert changed his life; John Muir spent months wandering over it, entranced. Some visitors included it among the Wonders of the World, and one travel writer gave up trying to describe the variety of colors he saw and settled on a more visceral image. "A chameleon," wrote William Hamilton Nelson, "would naturally explode in this desert trying to change to all these colors."

But today those colors have faded from our collective memory, and even some locals have forgotten where to find the desert. On one assignment I pulled off the highway at Winslow, on the edge of the Painted Desert, and took a seat at a café counter. The waitress poured coffee for the truck driver next to me.

"I was going to ask how you are," she told him, "but I won't bother. I can already tell by looking."

She started filling my cup, and I asked her what she thought was the best part of the Painted Desert.

"Where the hell's the Painted Desert?" she asked.

"It's the same thing as the Petrified Forest," the truck driver said. "Keep driving east, and you'll run into it."

The Painted Desert isn't a corner of Petrified Forest National Park; the park lies within the wider desert. To add to the confusion, botanists have classified it as a section of a much larger intermountain semidesert. I see it differently. The first ones to cross it on foot and horseback had it right. They encountered a landscape with a character so distinct, they recognized the Painted Desert as its own place.

On reaching the Ward Terrace, Dave and I stop to get our bearings. Before us runs a line of cliffs forming an unbroken front forty miles long. Only a few horse trails descend it, and these are rarely used anymore. The farthest cliffs dissolve into grainy blues as a light wind drags across the expanse below them. Every journey has a true beginning somewhere beyond the starting point. It may be a geographical divide, a cultural boundary, or simply this—a threshold of pure distance and light.

Dave's German shepherd, Mali, runs with her nose to the ground and doesn't slow until Dave sets up his tripod. She takes a seat next to him, ears perked, and looks out across the barrens where the camera points. Raw layers of red, orange, and bone white lie exposed to the elements along the weathered face of the escarpment. When paleontologist Lester Ward explored the Painted Desert in the 1890s, he reported that this region of painted cliffs had not only given the desert its name but in many respects rivaled the Grand Canyon.

Winds alone seem to thrive here. In calm weather they take the form of dust devils whirling at a distance. In stormy weather they pull horizontally across miles of bare ground to suddenly explode in clouds of dust towering over the highest cliffs. Driving rains come at long intervals, leaving the steady work to the winds. Water has rough cut the broad features of the terrain, but the wind shapes its character, reworking the surface in its own image. Bursts of air abrade the outcropping rocks into aerodynamic lines, weathering them into teardrop-shaped hummocks and transforming the sandstone to living dunes.

In the distance stand clusters of rock spires and misshapen knobs. Hoodoos. Spend time among the wind-carved rocks, and you will see how shifting light plays across them, unlocking whatever forms lie hidden in the human imagination. As the shadows grow, the faces emerge. Hoodoo was originally a form of folk magic practiced mainly by African Americans in the South. The wider society began using the term as slang for a spell, a jinx, or something haunted. Cowboys in the 1880s used it to mean spooky, and geologists found it useful when describing the strange lithic forms they encountered. For more familiar monoliths they fell back on architectural terms such as column, pillar, and turret. But these desert rocks have been worn and weathered into shapes which existed long before temple and palace. And they will be here long after.

Dave shifts his camera, and Mali adjusts her position to match. Looking in the same direction, I see a solitary hoodoo rising at the foot of the far cliffs. Even at a distance Brown's Spire stands as a visible landmark on the edge of Dinosaur Canyon, a wide and shallow amphitheater scooped from the cliff face. To reach it we'll need to find the right wash in a veining of washes.

Back in the trucks we veer southeast, paralleling the Adeii Eechii Cliffs. Curious about the name, I once asked Herbert Benally, a professor from Diné College on the reservation, what it meant. He had been talking with some men who spoke Navajo as their first language, and the three of them tried various pronunciations until the effort left them laughing. In spoken Navajo, the meaning of a word can change radically depending on the in-

Brown's Spire, Dinosaur Canyon

flection given to it. "We don't know what it means exactly," he said, "but we think it's something dirty." Later Danny Blackgoat, a Navajo-language instructor, gave it a shot. After rejecting several variations, he finally said it referred to "a pile of excrement that keeps building higher," a fitting image of the knobby mounds of siltstone found here.

The pitch and jerk of the truck adds a rough edge to the distance covered. Aiming for the prominent hoodoo, I turn up a wash; it soon narrows between cutbanks, leaving only enough room to squeeze through. And then it cliffs out. Turning the pickup around in a wide spot, standard procedure before parking, I shut it down. Dave pulls in, and we continue on foot across sand ridges and benches of bare sandstone. Red on yellow under a blue sky.

As Dave and I move closer, the standing rock looms ahead, rising more than forty feet above a base of tumbled boulders laced with white striations. Dave sets up as I circle the base, reading the names of paleontologists carved into it. From New York to Berkeley, the bone hunters have made their pilgrimage to this corner of the desert. Ned Colbert of Ghost Ranch fame signed in, as did R. T. Bird and Sam Welles, who discovered the first *Dilophosaurus* fossils north of here. And the man who began the tradition left this inscription: "B. Brown Am. Museum Nat. Hist. New York." With the letters already fading, another hundred years of dust storms will erase the register completely.

The greatest bone hunter in his day, Barnum Brown had his share of adventures while on collecting trips for the American Museum of Natural

History. He once fell into the crater of an extinct volcano, and on another expedition became shipwrecked and marooned off Tierra del Fuego. His knack for finding fossils gave rise to a rumor that he could sniff them out. Whatever method he used, Barnum did discover the first bones of *Tyrannosaurus rex*. Even in the field, the museum curator insisted on working in style. An old photograph shows him inspecting a rock exposure, nattily dressed in a tie and a long fur coat. The dapper scientist had the reputation of being a ladies' man among some geologists, who still refer to the hoodoo as "Brown's Phallus."

## on location

**D**ave and I leave the spire and continue to the foot of the cliffs, climbing onto a terrace studded with weathered outcrops. We have reached the site where an old movie was filmed. Called *The Painted Desert,* it was shot on location and starred Clark Gable in his first major Hollywood role. It was almost his last. Before the filming ended, actors were running for their lives when a simulated disaster suddenly turned real.

In 1930 this pocket of desert was even more remote and roadless than now. The film made here featured William Boyd, who went on to greater fame as Hopalong Cassidy, while Clark Gable played the heavy. From the start, bad luck plagued the film. A cattle drive turned into a stampede, stunt men broke bones, and a flash flood compounded their troubles.

Near the end of the filming, director Howard Higgin ordered his explosives expert to detonate two tons of gunpowder and dynamite for the film's climatic scene. The charges were placed to trigger a spectacular rock slide meant to bury a mine tunnel right after the miners had escaped. Timing was critical. As movie cameras began to roll, the powder boss threw the switch and sent 100 tons of rock skyward in a explosion of unexpected force. The special effects crew had miscalculated the hardness of the rock with disastrous results.

Extras scrambled over each other trying to squeeze out of the tunnel. Those outside were knocked off their feet by the concussion, and they got up running as huge boulders crashed down. "I looked up and saw thousands of rocks coming down out of the air," the director said. Rocks, hurled up 500 feet, fell among the crowd of spectators and crushed four cars parked a half mile away. A 100-pound boulder almost hit Clark Gable. "Stones as large as grand pianos were blown a mile," he recounted. "One man was killed and twenty-eight were injured. I was knocked down by a tornado of loose dirt, but no rock touched me."

The explosion blew the cameramen off a platform and destroyed all but one of their cameras. William Wallace, a former Rough Rider wounded at the Battle of San Juan Hill, was knocked unconscious with a badly fractured skull. The first man to reach him thought he was dead. The tough old rancher, who worked as a driver, eventually recovered; but soundman Frank Gailand died of head injuries after being flown back to California.

Believing the film jinxed, the codirector cancelled the shoot, and most of the cast immediately returned to Hollywood by train. Only seventy-five feet of film was salvaged, but enough remained for theater audiences to watch a scene where men were actually running for their lives.

The old reports mentioned a last, undetonated charge. Before leaving the set, the powder boss ordered the wires to it severed to prevent another accident. The chances were good it had been left in place when the filming ended.

As I now search the foot of the cliff, I find where the cameras once stood directly in front of what remains of the mine tunnel. The local Navajo salvaged anything useful years ago, but left the mangled sheets of metal and splintered wood half buried among the rocks. As I inspect a heavy-gauge metal barrel, crushed flat and twisted by the blast, Dave approaches. "It looks like an airplane crash," he says.

I work my way up the slope, carefully checking the debris, and soon find two sticks of dynamite lying on the surface. They resemble weathered scrolls of parchment beginning to unravel. It must be part of the charge that hadn't detonated. I resist the urge to pick one up, knowing how unstable old dynamite can be. These sticks have been lying around for three-quarters of a century.

Boulder, Moenave Formation

We start back to the trucks, and within a few paces no evidence remains of the events that unfolded here. Centuries of winds have swept the desert clean, leaving only a scattered history. A few sandblasted potsherds, an abandoned hogan or two, and a stick of old dynamite from a staged disaster that became what it had tried to imitate. As a line from another movie, *The Matrix,* put it: "Welcome to the desert of the real."

# the dinosaur dancehall

**W**hen I first began exploring the desert, the pressure was on. I had made a promise to my son and had to find a way to deliver. At the age of four, Erik talked dinosaurs nonstop during the day. At night he dreamed of dinosaurs under the wings of a pterodactyl model hanging from his bedroom ceiling. One of his chief pleasures was to carefully correct my pronunciation of dinosaur names.

This fine obsession, I thought, would run its course, but as the months piled up there was no end in sight. One evening we went to a dinosaur lecture at the Museum of Northern Arizona. When the slides ended and the lights came on, the speaker had all the children put their names in a hat for door prizes. There was a dinosaur cap and a dinosaur T-shirt, but the ultimate prize was a chunk of real dinosaur bone. Like every kid in the room, Erik never wanted anything more in his whole life.

"Your chances are slim," I warned. "Don't get your hopes up."

"I won't," he said. But when the last name was drawn and it wasn't his, he had to fight back the tears.

"Don't worry," I said, trying to comfort him, and without realizing what I was doing blurted out, "I'll find you your own dinosaur bone."

It was one of those rash promises a father sometimes makes and immediately regrets. I had no idea where to start looking, but with my credibility at stake I began asking around. A geologist mentioned a place where he thought dinosaur fossils had turned up long ago. It wasn't on the maps.

"Head north into the Painted Desert," he said, "and take a right turn. You can't miss it."

On one of the early attempts to find it, I pulled over to stretch my legs. A raven perched on a rock nearby, its head turned at a right angle. One eye looked straight at me, while the other scanned the empty horizon. After miles of dirt road driving, I'd seen a lone cow searching for a clump of grass and a deserted hogan. The rest was pure desert.

Before reaching Black Falls Crossing on the Little Colorado, I caught a glimpse to the north of cliffs crazily weathered and burning red in the evening light. They appeared remote, rising from a terrace cut off from the rest of the landscape by a lower band of cliffs. I returned to the truck and rushed along the graded road, looking for a way in. To have a chance of reaching them before dark, I needed to hurry.

Near the river a road branched off, paralleling the cliffs at a distance. I followed it. Moving at a good clip, the truck stirred up a tail of dust and bumped over cutbanks at each wash. Soon I passed a hogan with some life to it. A few sheep grazed on sparse tufts of grass near an old engine block resting on a stump of petrified wood. Two skittish horses galloped away when they heard the truck approach.

A faint track led toward a break in the cliffs, and I took it. Topping a rise, I met a pickup inching along with patches of paint worn to bare metal by years of grit-laced winds. A grandmother wearing a headscarf sat at the wheel, herding a few scraggly sheep with the help of a man who walked alongside to keep them bunched together. When I stopped to let them pass, he ambled over, looking puzzled.

"What's a white man doing way out here?" he asked slowly, unused to translating his thoughts into English.

"Looking at the red rocks," I told him.

"Yes," he said in Navajo, glancing over his shoulder at the cliffs. Satisfied with the answer, he returned to his sheep.

The track faded as quickly as the light was leaving the sky. With no time to continue, I parked the truck and climbed the side of an untracked dune. The air was so clear a light breeze carried the smell of snow from the San Francisco Peaks fifty miles to the south. The sun, balanced on the horizon far to the southwest, ignited the colored bands of rock for one long, burning moment. And then suddenly the darkness fell like a hatch closing.

When my friend Scott Milzer arrived in town a few weeks later, I enlisted his aid in the bone hunt. He had just spent six months on a fishing boat in Alaska and was eager to have a chance to wander through the desert. Erik had sent him a drawing of pterodactyls flying over a boat, and Milzer had hung it up in the galley for good luck. Now the pterodactyls had come home to roost.

"I'm ready to bring those dinosaurs to their knees," he boasted, pacing the floor. "We'll do nothing less than push back the paleontological envelope. I'm talking about finding a dinosaur, a *Smilodon*, with a spear in its ribs." Erik cut in to remind him that a *Smilodon* was a saber-toothed tiger not a dinosaur, but Milzer's enthusiasm went unchecked. "By the time we return," he continued, "the Friends of the Mesozoic will be begging us to join."

After miles of touch-and-go driving, we topped the first escarpment. A faint track followed the upper terrace and skirted a fossil site I had found on an earlier trip. At this spot dinosaur coprolites were washing out of the soft rock. Milzer and I weren't exactly experts, but we knew a coprolite when we saw one—millions of years hadn't changed the look of a turd. These were surprisingly small, about the size of something that might turn up in a cat box. My friend was disappointed. "I'm holding out for at least paperweight size," he said. "Or if I find one with the right color, I'll use it for a bola tie."

That evening the skies threatened, and the wind picked up. After making camp I sat in the truck trying to catch the weather report, not wanting to get caught out here in a heavy rain. I wasn't able to find anything local but did catch an ad skipping in from Utah. It was an attempt to lure housewives away from their soap operas by selling them ironing-time inspirational tapes. I double-checked to make sure the key was turned off when I finished. A dead battery would mean a day's walk to get help.

Milzer heated water on a stove behind a windbreak, and I took a seat nearby with my back propped against an ancient sand dune turned to stone. Fossil dunes clustered around us like a chain of islands surrounded by a flat sea of wind-polished agates. The nearby dunes caught the fiery glow of the low sun as the farther cliffs flared up in apocalyptic reds.

Early the next morning, we set out to find a dinosaur tracksite first investigated by Barnum Brown. But the legendary paleontologist never published a report on it. Over the years sands covered the tracks, and the location was lost.

Barnum first came to the Painted Desert in 1904 with Lester Ward and was lured back by Hollywood producer Gilbert Gable. The filmmaker bankrolled an expedition to study the dinosaur tracksite discovered by Frank Goldtooth, a local Navajo leader. In 1929 Barnum was scrabbling around Dinosaur Canyon, searching for old bones and fossil tracks. While he was in the field, a controversy broke wide open.

A wire story, picked up by the Arizona newspapers, claimed the expedition was planning to hack out the dinosaur tracks and ship them back east.

Horse skull, dead zone

Alerted by the report, Arizona governor John Phillips ordered the county sheriff to take action if necessary to protect the ancient remains. He wasn't overreacting. For years archeologists had been shipping prehistoric artifacts by the train-car load back to eastern museums and wealthy collectors. Two years before, New York cotton broker Charles Bernheimer removed slabs of rock containing dinosaur tracks from a remote canyon and sent them back to the American Museum of Natural History. During the same period, a Smithsonian geologist, with permit in hand, collected 1,700 pounds of fossil tracks from Grand Canyon National Park. Another party of well-heeled fossil hunters in the Painted Desert naturally raised suspicions.

Sheriff Jack Kester tracked down Barnum and his patron only to find them innocently taking photographs of the site. By then they knew questions were being raised in the papers. Gable expressed his surprise that the governor had confused them with vandals and pothunters, and assured the lawman they would only take plaster casts. The crisis subsided, and except for his name carved in sandstone Barnum left nothing behind to mark the expedition.

In 1986 Scott Madsen, a paleontologist from the Museum of Northern Arizona, decided to find the lost tracksite. He packed his standard lunch of chocolate cupcakes, to be washed down with chocolate milk, and then went to hunt Barnum's tracks. Accompanied by his friend Keith Becker, he took along an old photo of the site from the 1930s. By matching up the skyline, Madsen narrowed the search area considerably, and his knowledge of the terrain soon led him to the right cluster of hoodoos. Convinced it was the original site, they cleared away a layer of sand and soon dozens of tracks began to appear. They had uncovered the Dinosaur Dancehall.

Milzer was skeptical about Barnum Brown's discovery, not trusting anybody named after P. T. Barnum, but he played along. "A journey of a thousand miles," he said, "always starts off on the wrong foot."

The two of us followed a dry wash and climbed a cliff at its head. Surrounded by hoodoos we crossed an exposure of bare rock and quickly spotted the three-toed tracks. A drift of sand hid many of them, but those still exposed were remarkably distinct, showing the sharp claw marks of carnivores. During her study of the site, Grace Irby counted more than 300 tracks, with many of them grouped in trackways with multiple strides. Some of the dinosaurs were walking, some were trotting, and several showed rare running gaits. She was able to calculate a top speed of nearly nineteen miles per hour for the swiftest dinosaur.

And this action took place millions of years in the past. These red siltstones and sandstones came from wind-laid sands and rivers meandering across floodplains. The interfingered deposits, known as the Moenave Formation, date to between 185 million and 195 million years old. To stretch the imagination that far back in time is difficult for most of us. But for George Billingsley, a geologist with the U.S. Geological Survey, the rock holds all the clues needed to bring these ancient environments alive. The geological record indicates shallow sheets of sand and small dunes increasing in thickness as you travel to the east.

"Looking farther east and northeast," he said, "you would probably see

Dinosaur tracks, Goldtooth site

distant sand dunes that were forming the Wingate Sandstone. Looking north, northwest, and perhaps west you would see the shallow, distant seaways or tidal flats of the retreating Chinle seas."

Hopi petroglyphs were pecked into a cliff near the dinosaur prints. These clan symbols show a sun next to a lunar crescent, a rain cloud, and a shield design representing the center of the universe, the place where the Hopi now live. A few scratchings were added to the panel at a later time, including a pair of bird tracks which might refer to the Navajo name for the site, *tsidii nabitiin* "place of the bird tracks." Some Hopi believe this type of track belongs to Kwaatoko, a bird standing as tall as a man. When prayed to in times of crisis, the bird swoops into battle to defend the Hopi. "There is a debate about the footprints," said Delfred Leslie, a traditional leader from First Mesa. "Some Hopi say it's Kwaatoko, the man war-bird. It resembles a prehistoric creature, a flesh eater, and it's used by a warrior society. Others are not so sure."

We began hiking back to camp, taking a roundabout way to look for more tracks. I crossed a dry wash and noticed an unusual chunk of rock. Unlike the surrounding stone, it had the smooth surface and grainy center of a fossil bone. Focused on tracks, I had almost missed it. I followed the trail of fragments up the wash to an outcrop where intact bones were eroding from the red Moenave Formation. It had to be a dinosaur.

Back in town, Madsen identified a fossil from the site as being the tail vertebrae from a dinosaur. But he was skeptical about whether it had come from the Moenave, since it's easy to confuse the rock layers. And there was another problem—the only known fossils from the Moenave were some fish scales and bones from *Protosuchus,* a creature resembling a crocodile. At that time, no dinosaur bones had been found in the Moenave. Milzer had to catch a plane the next day, so I arranged with Madsen to return to the bone site a week later. I brought my son along to make good on my promise.

We parked as close as possible and walked the last half mile. Madsen said the Navajo call this area *tsénidoōlzhai,* "upward-projecting rocks strewn about." As we got closer, the paleontologist's excitement grew; we were definitely in the Moenave. When he saw the bluish-white bone actually embedded in the rock, he couldn't hold back. "This is amazing!" he said. "Excellent!" Paleontologists have trouble hiding their enthusiasm.

Erosion had exposed rib fragments and vertebrae, and as Madsen brushed away the dirt he became more convinced it was an unknown species of dinosaur. The animal had died about 190 million years ago in an arroyo, much like the wash we had driven up to reach the site. Madsen wanted to keep digging but restrained himself, knowing it had to be done right or the scientific value might be lost. We would leave the bones in place.

Meanwhile, Erik had dropped to his hands and knees to search for fossil fragments. He resembled a beagle on a scent as he crawled along in a floppy-eared dog hat with his head bent low. Suddenly he stood up and threw his arms in the air. "I wouldn't want to be anywhere else in the whole world," he said.

I knew what he meant. Americans are a restless people, always searching for something different, something better. But every once in a while we fall into a moment when nothing is lacking. Standing in the middle of a vast expanse with only rock and sand as far as the eye could see, the two of us had all we could want.

## Goldtooth camp

Continuing south along Ward Terrace, Dave and I turn up a dry wash marked by the recent tracks of Jack Goldtooth's car. The sheepherder, born in a hogan on the rim above, has spent most of his life in the desert, and I check in with him whenever I pass through.

We stop our trucks in front of his old trailer, set up on blocks, and wait. Rather than knock on the door, the custom is to sit patiently or honk—take your pick. A Geo Tracker sits nearby, the back half of the roof cut off to make it easier for loading saddles and bags of grain. Recently Jack had moved his

Hoodoo garden near Goldtooth camp

trailer to higher ground to get closer to better grazing, I thought. It turned out he only wanted to get better cell phone reception.

The Navajo steps out after a long moment, and we shake hands with a light touch. A greeting shouldn't be rushed, and we talk casually for a while. His nearest neighbor lives fifteen miles away, and he likes it that way. "It's real peaceful," he says. "Nobody around." He told me the trader from Cameron used to bring tourists out here a long time ago. "No one," he said, "comes here any more."

Having closer contact with the elements than with people, he has seen his share of droughts, flash floods, a tornado or two, and dust storms. About ten years ago, a massive wall of dust came rolling in when he was out with his sheep. "There was nothing you could do," he remembers, "nowhere to go." It was followed by a year of blowing sand caused, he believes, by the death of an important Hopi priest. "Those big, big honchos, they have the super-power, the Source."

Two years ago I met Jack when taking a group of paleontologists to the dinosaur bone site. We were driving up the wash when I spotted a Navajo keeping watch on his sheep from a high dune. We stopped the truck, and I climbed up to let him know what we were doing. The sheepherder was packing a pistol, unusual for a Navajo, and I noticed his toes sticking out from a pair of worn boots. He introduced himself, and we talked about the lack of grass and how the recent rains would help. Most of the nearby washes had flooded and a few playas had recharged. "Lots of water," he said. "It will take two weeks for the grass to come up after the rain."

I asked if he knew of other places with dinosaur remains. "Yes," he said, "lots of those tracks way over there. Go down that wash. You have a four-wheel drive? Go right up that sand dune. Go way over there, cross that other wash, and follow that ridge. There's wild horses over that way. Take a left, and right there by that rock that looks like a hogan, right there on a flat rock are all those tracks." We could spend a day driving in circles and still not find it.

"Can you take us there?"

"*Aoo*," he said, agreeing to guide us when we returned. He headed back to his camp, and the four of us continued to Barnum's tracks. Will Downs, a freelance paleontologist, knew this area well. He had prospected for fossils throughout the area and found the remains of what at that time was the oldest mammal in the Western Hemisphere. Barry Albright began his career as an underwater paleontologist and now found himself high and dry in the desert Southwest. Dave Gillette, the former state paleontologist for Utah, had discovered and excavated *Seismosaurus,* the world's longest dinosaur. Dave and Barry were curators of paleontology and geology at the Museum of Northern Arizona but dropped what they were doing for a chance to get into the field. A good sign.

We inspected the dinosaur tracksite, and after some note taking and a GPS reading, walked over to the Moenave bone site. "This needs to be excavated," Barry said after a quick survey, knowing how rare fossils are from this formation. Behind us, Will was on the scent, checking bone fragments and the angle at which they disappeared into the bedrock. "It's a good site," he announced and pulled out a bottle of Paleo-Bond, squirting the superglue on the surface bones to slow the weathering. Dave wanted to make the excavation of the site a top priority and studied the terrain to see if a truck could reach it. "If you can't drive to it," he said with a smile, "it's not a site."

Back at the Goldtooth camp, Jack climbed in the front seat of our truck, having corralled his sheep. He asked Barry which way he wanted to go.

"The shortest," he answered.

Jack took that to mean the most direct way, but it wasn't the quickest. We zigged and zagged for a couple of miles, up sand ridges and down washes, skirting mudholes and crossing one dune after another. Jack directed Barry along a faint set of intermittent tire tracks, telling him to turn left and right so often I gave up trying to remember the route. It became a classic rez road trip. A pair of pronghorn disappeared over a ridge, and Jack told us a hundred antelope live here year-round.

"Do you hunt them?" I asked.

"No, I let them grow."

Finally we reached the site, a patch of bare rock in a sandy wash, and in a moment we were walking over dinosaur footprints. To our surprise, it was a major tracksite. The rock had preserved a concentration of three-toed prints displaying fine detail—heel marks, foot pads, and claws long and lethal. Most of the tracks were about the size of an open hand, and a few smaller ones were left by infants. At times runoff washes over the site, filling some of the impressions with a mosaic of pebbles. An expert tracker, the Navajo told me these animals had been milling about at water, and taking a closer look I knew he was right. I asked him what type of animal left these prints, curious to see what he might come up with. "I'm not sure. The hip was about here," he said, holding his hand a little below his waist, "and stood this high."

Dave Gillette watched the Navajo closely as he held an arm above his head, indicating a height of about seven feet. The paleontologist agreed with his estimate. Encouraged, Jack commented on how people long ago lived on the nearby buttes to escape the dinosaurs. The prehistoric sites on top of them convinced him dinosaurs and humans had once coexisted, an idea likely reinforced by the traditional Monster Slayer stories he had grown up hearing.

As the paleontologist jotted down a few lines in his all-weather notebook, he told Jack he was naming the tracksite after him. We continued combing the site and found an impressive number of fossil prints. More than 500 of them crisscrossed the outcrop, and the potential existed for many more beneath the sand. "Why hasn't anyone found this site before?" the paleontologist wondered, and I gave him a straightforward answer.

"Nobody asked Jack."

All of us try to make sense out of the given world, and one puzzle faced by indigenous people was how to account for fossils. In 1884 ethnographer Frank Cushing related a story told to him by the Zuni.

"In the days of creation," he wrote, "the world was too damp and many great beings destructive to men and the creatures roamed abroad." The young war gods shot arrows of lightning over the four regions of earth to make it habitable. "The waters receded, the earth was dried, the shells and monsters of the great waters, many ferocious beings and prey beasts were changed to stone, or shriveled and hardened . . . Hence on the mountains, in the ravines and valleys, among cliffs, we find strange forms of living beings in stone."

A mythic perspective comes easily in the desert. I find myself drawn to places where the normal sense of time collapses. In the Petrified Forest I have seen a prehistoric house built from petrified wood, and outside Laramie I used to drive by a cabin built of dinosaur bones. Out here the tracks of strange life-forms punch holes in the solid present, weakening its hold.

Dave Edwards and I leave Goldtooth's place and make camp in hoodoo country, across a wash from the ruins of a hogan. It was the home of Jack's father, Frank Goldtooth, the man who showed Barnum Brown the main dinosaur tracksite. Frank's reputation as a medicine man was well established through his practicing the Blessingway, Upward Reaching Way, and other ceremonials. He even had a cure for those who dreamed of falling into canyons and were unable to climb out.

I head off alone to explore the area before dark, walking among the hoodoos. White striations alternate with bands of red across the faces of the rock, all rounded and smoothed by the wind. I notice the stillness, and stop. Nothing stirs; the moment hangs suspended. The human spirit absorbs silence the way roots do water, but we live in an aural world and the lack of sound can be unsettling. Accustomed to a constant soundtrack, the body grows restless in its absence and turns inward, listening to its own voice.

Suddenly the sky takes a dramatic shift, saturating the landscape with a red wash. I face west, watching as the sun almost burns through the horizon before ending in a last throw of radiant light. Spend time in the desert, and it comes as no surprise to learn that the Zuni Indians pray not only for rain but for light.

## the blue wind

**M**omentum keeps the pickup from trenching into the sand as Dave takes it down the flank of a dune the next morning. We use a single truck to find a way into an intriguing section of cliffs. At the bottom he turns up the bed of a wash, dodging mudholes and bypassing rock shelves where resistant layers outcrop. Ahead lies the main scarp, banded like a Navajo blanket in reds, lavender, and bone white—a blanket with the edges unraveling in a wild tangle. A scrim of clouds softens the light as we head toward Paiute Trail Point.

Dunescape, Paiute Trail Point

Signs of a recent rain mark the desert. Floodwater has coursed down the arroyos leaving behind curling shards of mud, and green blades push through clumps of dead grass. During a long drought, the anchoring vegetation dies and the sands begin to move, choking the washes until the next cloudburst recuts the channel. Sand in a desert is permanent, water ephemeral. The wash tightens at the base of a crazily weathered monolith, tapering to an apex sixty feet above us. Sand dunes sweep up one side of a shallow canyon ahead and cliffs bookend the other.

Parking his truck, Dave pulls out the camera gear as Mali takes off with her nose to the ground, reading spoor at a trot. Ahead of us, a falling dune has buried the cliff face, and a trail angles up the point. For centuries the winds have blown from the southwest, tossing dust thousands of feet in the air and bouncing grains of sand along the surface. Dune joins dune until a wave of sand breaks against the windward cliffs and steadily climbs the far side of the long promontory. On top, the dunes keep moving, cascading down the leeward face in steep fans and creating a way through the cliffs.

I head out, picking up the trail where it cuts across a bend of the wash. Hoodooed walls rise 300 feet on each side, the red Moenave taking on an orange cast in this light. Incised by runoff and wind scoured, the rock walls have the knobby texture of Indian corn, a mutant strain. A horse has punched staggered holes in the sand slope where the trail begins to climb, and I plant my feet in them, following a distinct path. This is the route of the old Moqui Trail.

In 1881 Frank Cushing set out from Zuni to visit the Havasupai Indians in the Grand Canyon. The Smithsonian anthropologist had become intrigued by stories of a people who lived in a canyon so deep, he was told, the sun reached the bottom only at midday. The journey would be difficult, and his Zuni friends refused to accompany him at first. Only after gaining a leadership position in their society was he able to convince someone to guide him. By then it was summer, the wrong time to be crossing a desert. Cushing insisted on going, though the journey would nearly cost him his life: they ran out of water before returning.

With three Indian companions, Cushing followed a beaten path into the Painted Desert, a route known as the Supai Trail for those heading west and the Moqui Trail for those eastbound. Moqui was a Spanish term for the Hopi, picked up from the Pueblo Indians in New Mexico. When Cushing reached a rim overlooking the desert, he noted in his journal "a wild, sublime series of terraces cut into a thousand fanciful forms by wind and rain." With his Indian guides, he descended "over a beautiful cliff of red and brilliant pink sandstone" before reaching an extensive dunefield. The next year he described the same scene for the *Atlantic Monthly*.

"Terrace after terrace," he wrote,

one below another, stretched out before me, melting off into misty mirages. Citadels, towers, rancherias, green, sunny bases, appeared to be before me. Giant sand-dunes rose from plains of blazing, dazzling white. Here and there, near and far, rose great solitary rocks, angular as if the sculptor's chisel had clearly cut them, and gorgeous with chrome and pink. Everywhere over this mighty scene were wafted clouds and clouds of sand, which shimmered, golden and rosy, in the evening sun. Everything in the scene gave the false impression of intense past activity: fallen rocks; sublime depths of cañon; great basins; high, flat peaks; immense sandy plains, which looked as if they had been lifted and thrown upon their rocky heights, or cast into their sombre depths, where the winds of centuries had played with them daily. Of all this activity, with no sound, only great whirling, waving, drifting clouds of sand remained.

On his return to Zuni from the Grand Canyon expedition, Cushing brought with him an Apache scalp. Many of his colleagues already thought the pioneer ethnologist had descended into savagery by living with the people he studied, an innovation which later became standard procedure. Their suspicions seemed to be confirmed when word spread of his having taken the enemy scalp, a requirement for initiation into an important warrior society. Cushing never directly admitted the killing, and he left his written accounts of the incident vague, allowing readers to believe what they wanted. Since the Zuni priests only accepted his claim after he threatened to leave the pueblo and return to Washington, they may have decided he was more useful to them as a Zuni insider than a government official with a grudge.

Some historians believe Coronado's soldiers used the Moqui Trail in 1540. Guided by Hopi Indians they headed west in search of the Colorado

River, and on their way bumped into the Grand Canyon. By 1910 most of the trail had been abandoned, and soon cattle and trucks obliterated any traces the rains had not washed out.

Early descriptions of the route led me to suspect Cushing had crossed the Painted Desert somewhere in this area. Historians have usually placed the trail in the Moenkopi Wash farther north or the Dinnebito Wash to the south, but I thought Paiute Trail Point might be the key. Jack Goldtooth confirmed this when he told me it had been used mainly by Havasupai and Hualapai on their way to trade with the Hopi. James Peshlakai, whose family has a sheep camp nearby, was more emphatic. "They got the name wrong on the map," he told me. "It's the Supai Trail." And referring to the earliest Spanish explorations, he added, "That's the way the conquistadores went!"

The trail I'm now following soon breaches the rim of the promontory, extending in a long landing from the higher plateau. From this vantage point, Cushing had described the scene below, now spreading out like a painted canvas layered with light. The only part he missed was the strangeness of it. I find the landscape more otherworldly than images sent back from the deserts of Mars.

"Every time I come out here," Dave says when we meet up again, "it confirms just how wild and remote it is."

A storm system has been trying to coalesce since midmorning, with falls of dry rain and dark clouds lowering to the north. Not wanting to get stranded high up the wash, we turn back. At a rocky stretch we are forced to clear a path, tipping boulders out of the way and walking out the route to

Storm approaching a dunefield

check the angle of approach. Where the streambed widens, Dave pulls the truck onto a flat outcrop and stops. Lunchtime.

He drops the tailgate and sets out a feast. The beer first, of course, followed by a salad, every ingredient fresh, organic, and hand selected. Then he instructs me in preparing the main course—a whole-wheat tortilla slathered with cream cheese, topped with a cucumber sliced Julienne style, and wrapped around a chunk of smoked Alaskan salmon the size of a dog's ear. Having spent years in remote places, Dave knows how to take care of himself.

Winds have sanded smooth the rock we sit on, exposing a scattering of concretions. Each has a tail of sandstone tapering away on the leeward side, the way sand drifts behind brush. On exposed faces nearby the rock has been sandblasted into projecting prongs, while a sandstone outcrop on the open flat has taken on the shape of a capsized boat, weathered into a smooth-sided yardang.

Back on the main track, where no one has driven recently, we turn south toward an extensive dunefield. On the cliff side, a band of wild horses takes off at a run, stringing out behind the leader. In a single pulse they flow across the crest of a dune, silhouetted for a moment against the sky before disappearing. Waves of pure sand rise in the distance. The road soon reaches the first dune and disappears under the sand where advancing dunes have buried the old tracks. We take a detour and skirt a line of dunes whose hollow sides climb steeply at the angle of repose.

Leaving the truck, Dave and I set out on foot. Behind us a dust devil augers across the surface of the desert at such a distance it appears to move at a languid pace. Dave sets up his tripod on the crest line and aims his camera north, catching the white sand against a surge of storm-blue clouds. On the far horizon I notice dust exploding in white plumes 300 feet high along a front several miles wide. A dust storm is heading our way.

The air is still for a long moment, and then I notice a stirring. The surface of the dune begins to move as grains of sand shift. Soon the skin of the dune turns kinetic, vibrating hypnotically as the wind picks up. To the north, the line of rising dust is moving incredibly fast, chewing up ground at the rate of about fifty miles an hour. In a few minutes it will be upon us, and I can hear a roaring in the distance long before the wind arrives. Waiting until the last minute Dave packs up his camera, preparing for what is about to break loose.

The sky darkens, and a stray tumbleweed cartwheels along the ground, outracing the storm. And then another flies past and another. The wall of dust nears as tendrils of sand flow up the side of the dune and streamers of sand blow across the flats. Suddenly the winds hit full force, and the air temperature takes a sudden dive. My clothes flap violently, and my hair whips about as dust is being sucked skyward.

Among the Navajo each direction has a different wind associated with it, such as the Blue Wind and the Yellow Wind. Some weavers in the western reservation also work wind symbols into their rugs. In each corner of a Storm Pattern design they weave a figure which some have interpreted as

Narrowleaf yucca in shifting sand

representing the house of the wind, a force they know well. The Painted Desert is the most windswept corner of Arizona, where extreme winds have repeatedly blown the caps off anemometers.

Turning my back to the gale, I retreat to the truck. I dive into the front seat and watch as the storm sweeps past. We are parked between the curving points of a barchan dune, which takes its name from the Kazakh word for ram's horn. Dave sits staring at the slip face, mesmerized by the grains blowing across it. The force of the wind triggers tongues of cascading sand, which are almost instantly wiped smooth. Since prevailing winds play the primary role in shaping dunes, I thought a crosswind would only blunt its forward motion. But this storm, hitting at a perpendicular angle, spurs the dune's incremental advance.

In a few minutes, the wall of dust along the leading edge has blown past, but the wind remains strong. It combs the dunes, stirring the sand into curlers along the highest crest and causing a hypnotic agitation along the slip face. Returning to the main road, Dave has to break trail where sand has drifted over our tracks and left streamers trailing behind each clump of grass. The storm has already begun the process of covering any trace of our passage. We cross the desert like a boat on the water, leaving only a momentary wake.

That evening my thoughts shift about like grains of sand, windblown and unconsolidated. I think about deserts and madness. My earliest memory of the desert comes from watching a Saturday morning cartoon as a kid. In it, a crazed prospector takes a broad brush and manically slops bright colors on every surface as he transforms the drab hills into a Technicolor wonderland. He finishes by banging in a sign that reads, "The Painted Desert." Ever since, the desert has reminded me of terrain gone slightly mad. Thomas Wolfe picked up on this theme when he drove across the Painted Desert in the summer of 1938. Conditions could be punishing before air-conditioning, and the novelist suffered from the intense heat. All around him the rock landscape transformed into what he called, "the demented reds."

Every desert needs a madman, someone to fill the emptiness with dreams and revelations. Peter Jonathan Edwards, a prophet of sorts, was considered half-crazed by the Mormon settlers. He wandered about the Painted Desert in the 1870s with a heavy muzzle loader over his shoulder and a few possessions wrapped in an oxhide. At isolated hogans he preached to the Navajo, his long hair streaming in the wind, and cornered the Hopi in their villages. Tolerant of the god-struck, they listened politely before sending him on his way. Their parched corn was a welcome respite from his usual diet of rabbit, packrat, and grasshopper.

In his travels Edwards came upon fossil bones and petrified wood eroding from the badlands, clear evidence of earlier life turned to stone. A revelation in the winter of 1879 convinced him he had discovered the site where Noah had dressed the timbers for his ark. Petrified wood chips littered the ground for all to see, and he was certain the fossil bones were the remains of animals destroyed in the great flood. And one night he dreamed of a boat in the desert, Noah's petrified ark waiting to be found on a high mesa top.

Thirst can also drive a person mad. It's easy to appreciate the beauty of

Wind-carved cliff, Ward Terrace

an arid landscape when I have enough food for a week, a bumper jack for deep sand, a pair of 2.5 gallon water kegs for insurance, and Dave's truck for a backup. But run short on water, and the desert shows another face.

"The scene was one of utter desolation," wrote Lieutenant Joseph C. Ives when probing the Painted Desert in 1858.

> Not a tree nor a shrub broke its monotony. The edges of the mesas were flaming red, and the sand threw back the sun's rays in a yellow glare. Every object looked hot and dry and dreary. The animals began to give out. We knew it was desperate to keep on, but felt unwilling to return, and forced the jaded brutes to wade through the powdery impalpable dust for fifteen miles. The country, if possible, grew worse . . . Even beyond the ordinary limit of vision were other bluffs and sand fields, lifted into view by the mirage, and elongating the hideous picture.

Forced by lack of water to leave "this condemned region," the lieutenant turned back to the river.

A scientific party lead by C. Hart Merriam, director of the U.S. Biological Survey, crossed the Painted Desert in the summer of 1889. On the third day a flash flood tore down Dinnebito Wash, burying the spring the scientists depended on. Unable to locate it under the mud, they pushed on and soon ran out of water. The naturalist observed the labored beating of his heart as his blood thickened, and he had difficulty recognizing familiar birds and animals due to the miragelike distortions. Merriam nearly died of thirst before an old Hopi found the party three days later. The Indian guided the scientists to water of sorts. He pointed to a mudhole, too dirty for their horses to drink, and stuck in an old rubber hose. Each mouthful of water he sucked out was spit into a pot. Finicky habits normally fall by the wayside in the desert, but before taking a drink Merriam boiled the pot of siphoned water and threw in a handful of coffee grounds. In his official report, he simply stated, "The heat was intense, and much suffering was occasioned by want of water."

The next morning I roll over to find the moon hanging in the western sky, a shave or two past full. This is the time when traditionals from Window Rock to Walpi stand facing east, and whatever lives—raven, coyote, flower—turns toward the point where the sun will rise. The air lies dead still without a stir of wind. The dark cliff line stands in sharp relief against the dawn sky, stretched so tight the air vibrates. As the sky lightens I follow the sun working down the face of the San Francisco Peaks to the south, moving across the Little Colorado, and finally striking the terrace below me. Suddenly a ray of sunlight breaks across the eastern rim with laser intensity, splitting sky from earth and flooding the camp with light.

## painted cliffs

**D**ave and I separate for a few hours. He needs to photograph, and I have a walk to take in memory of a friend. After studying the map, I drive up a wash which should bring me within a couple of miles of the target—the remains of a dinosaur. A narrow canyon parts the cliffs where rock walls flank both sides of the drainage. It only grows tighter as I near the head of navigation. At the next wide spot I turn around and park the truck, content to be on foot again. To reach the upper terrace, I need to find a way through the Red Rock Cliffs.

After checking three branches of the canyon, I come up with three dead ends and only spot the solution after returning to the pickup. It's not an obvious route. A combination of short pitches and a traverse takes me to a crumbly spur leading above. On top, I find myself on a point between arms of the canyon, right where I need to be. The skyline ahead matches my memory of the fossil site, and I head toward the outer tier of cliffs.

Half an hour later I contour along a band of a rock until finding a familiar slope. Gazing up I can make out the bones of a dinosaur eroding from the rock. It's a spectacular site. The nearly complete skeleton of a prosauropod curves over a bulge in the cliff rock, twisting upward the way a lizard climbs a sheer wall. The vertebrae resemble a fallen stack of poker chips and have the dark red cast of old iron. Stretched out, the dinosaur would reach a length of about five feet.

Two years ago Will Downs brought me here with two others. He had something he wanted to show us, something important. Will was a legend among paleontologists, the only full-time bone hunter in the world. Essentially self-taught, he was so good at finding fossils the top museums and universities in the country kept hiring him. He spent most of his time in exotic locales from Greenland to Uganda, and his fluency in Mandarin Chinese helped him negotiate with the Chinese authorities after getting arrested over permit difficulties. Only later did I learn why Will was so anxious for us to see his dinosaur site. He had cancer and knew he was dying. After keeping this place a secret for years, Will wanted to pass it on.

By late afternoon I've rendezvoused with Dave. He has been photo-

Electric storm, Red Rock Cliffs

graphing a canyon filled with fantastic hoodoos. It fingers back into the escarpment several miles in a stunning windscape of rock and sand. We decide to make camp at the foot of a prominent sentinel rock. Its broad base forms a pedestal for a sandstone horn weathered on the windward edge into duckbill projections. Behind it stands a rock wall as knobby as melted wax. No words match these rock forms. Architectural and anatomical analogies fail, literary allusions draw a blank, so we fall back on calling them hoodoos and let it go at that. Across the canyon a sand dune climbs to the rim, and an improbably balanced rock stands where the wash splits into two arms. Between rock and cliff lies sand, sand piled into dunes and rippled by currents of wind and water, sand anchored into hummocks by tufts of grass and yucca, sand drifting and flowing.

Exploring the area on foot, I watch the color of the rock change as the angle of sunlight shifts lower. Earlier at midday, the browns dominated the spectrum while the reds and oranges waited out the heat of day. With the sun now arcing west, the colors surface again, seeping from the pores of the rock in reds even more intense when set against the paint blue of the sky. As the shadows strengthen, the caprocks transform into sitting ducks, birds of prey, and flying saucers.

I circle back to where Dave has set up, and he tells me about a tree growing in the dry bed of the wash. Flash floods have deposited matted debris on the upstream side as high as his truck. Even with the evidence at hand, it's hard to imagine how instantly the weather can toggle from one extreme to the other. C. Hart Merriam experienced this on an August day in the

Wind-sculpted tower, Tohachi Wash

Painted Desert as he watched a rainstorm hammering the high mesas to the north. Where he stood, not a cloud passed between him and the sun. That night a loud roaring startled him. "In a moment," he wrote, "a great wave of thick mud rushed past with a tremendous roar, accompanied by a fetid stench." The leading edge of the flood, five feet high, swept down the dry wash and soon grew to a height of eight feet.

As Dave and I talk, dark clouds move in from the northeast, an unexpected direction. The cliffs have screened them until they're almost overhead. Wisps of dry rain hang suspended in the air, white against a backdrop of blue so dense it grades to black. Still catching light from the west, the cliffs glow blood red as a flush of color fills the air. Suddenly lightning spider-webs across the sky, and a few seconds later the first thunder I've heard in months rolls down the canyon. The two of us quickly rig for rain, pulling camp together and moving the trucks to higher ground. Just in case.

Currents of wind tumble over the cliffs and weave down the rock-cut channels, tangling together in shifting gusts, shaking the dry grass. In the falling air and the sudden cold, lightning strikes in an explosive flash and lingers as an afterimage on the retina. A moment later the storm lets loose, sweeping the ground with waves of rain.

The last light melts away to the west, too far away for the storm cell to obscure. We take shelter in the trucks and wait out the rain. Only one station comes in clear on the radio, and in the downpour I listen to KTNN out of Window Rock. The announcer interrupts a long run of Navajo with a few English fragments like "cash machine," letting me get the drift. Before long the intensity of the storm lessens. It has lasted long enough to send runoff flowing down the wash, but the canyon never flashes.

By morning, thick air has settled between the rows of cliffs and hangs even heavier when the damp sand begins to heat up. As I make coffee, we hear a truck approaching and soon see a pickup bouncing our way. It stops next to camp and a Navajo steps out, looking serious. Jerry Huskon lives in the hogan we passed yesterday at the mouth of the canyon. He keeps an eye on the place and wants to know what we're doing here. As I begin to explain, Dave mentions coming here before with a friend, James Peshlakai. "He's my clan brother," Jerry tells us. "You guys are okay."

## river road

**O**n the last day we begin our return to Cameron by circling back along the river. To get there we puzzle a way through the maze of one-track cow paths and two-track truck trails, bypassing a few homes clustered around a mission church.

Turning west before reaching Black Falls Crossing, Dave and I follow a graded road along the river. It follows a natural route through the northern Painted Desert taken by Mormon pioneers in covered wagons, outlaws and Indians on horseback, and even a band of scalp hunters. Its usefulness faded after the railroad came through northern Arizona in the 1880s and new towns bubbled up in its wake.

We make good time, rattling over the washboard surface. The ribbing forms when a truck hits a bump and the suspension absorbs the impact in a series of bounces. Once established, the pattern becomes entrenched with repeated use. After years of driving these roads, I've learned to take them at an optimal speed—too slow and the vehicle hits each rib with a jolt; too fast and it will shimmy and fishtail into the ditch. It's a rattling ride. The keys jiggle out of the ignition and land on the floor, while I clench my jaw to keep my teeth from chattering.

The first few miles of road cover a rolling expanse with enough grass some years to support a horse herd and cattle. A few families have managed to establish a toehold on the margins, but no one lives where the grass thins to a few clumps among the barren hills. I pass artifacts of earlier attempts at settlement—abandoned hogans, earth dams silted in or breached by flash floods, a line of stunted cottonwood trees planted for shade.

This land has its moods, which add to the beauty of the place. I have seen it in the cold months with ice on the river and in the dry months with the ground cracked like old shoe leather. I have looked across it without seeing an end to it, and have been caught up in blowing dust so thick I've had to climb a dune to see fifty feet ahead.

We cross sandy washes and skirt mounds of Chinle siltstones, the most characteristic formation in the Painted Desert. The rock is so soft, an outcrop twenty-five feet high can dissolve completely in a thousand years. At a

Barren hummock, Chinle Formation

distance the rock has the appearance of blue-gray clouds seen at dawn. Up close the powdery hummocks take on a lunar presence, a perfect location to fake a moon landing. Other pockets of Chinle rise up in colorful hills banded in maroon, green, and lavender. Pretty to look at, but after a hard rain the bentonite clays turn into supermud, coating tires with adobe retreads. At those times the locals wait it out; those who try pushing their luck end up waiting anyway, buried to their axles.

Territorial historian Sharlot Hall crossed the flooded river in 1911, a year before the bridge was completed, and narrowly avoided getting stuck in quicksand. Riding in a canvas-covered Studebaker wagon, she was on her way to collect the history of the Arizona Strip north of Grand Canyon. "All afternoon," she wrote, "we bore to the northeast and the country grew wilder . . . Near us the hills were topped with toad stools and caps and gnome-heads of harder clay, standing on slender necks that would fall in during some rain . . . The ground was shining in spots with the paint-like mud from yesterday's shower; I worked some of it up in my hands and it left them red as vermillion."

We pass old river terraces, sealed with a desert pavement of cobbles oxidized black and polished by the wind to a metallic glint. For centuries toolmakers have picked over the cherts, their flakes and rejected cores lying so thick in places they form a geologic layer of their own. Wait long enough, and the living become part of the stratigraphy. Across the river I spot buttes topped with Pueblo ruins; it's difficult at this distance to separate the masonry from the bedrock. Mounds of rubble and a few standing walls mark earlier occupations with the greatest concentration located in Wupatki National Monument.

Next to the monument, the CO Bar Ranch has a line cabin named River Camp. The cowboys sent to this bleak locale called it "Living Hell Ranch"—hot in summer, cold in winter, and a long way from any distractions. An older cabin, built in the 1880s, lies in a thicket nearby. To pass the time, cowhands carved brands into the wooden door jamb. In a few generations the brands will be as cryptic as the prehistoric petroglyphs nearby. Most of them are composites of simple shapes—bars, diamonds, letters—but the slightest variations once held great significance. A man could lose his life by altering a single line of a symbol—if it happened to be burned into the flank of a cow.

The landscape itself is encoded. There are signs everywhere: the track of the wind, the rock eroded into iconic shapes, the side of a dune crisscrossed with tiny trackways. Over time we choose new signs to follow. We now track the path of the planets with more precision than the trail of a stray horse.

Downriver stands a circular wall of stone, the remnants of a hogan built by Peshlakai Etsidi, an early Navajo leader. As a boy he fled from Ute raiders and U.S. soldiers, taking refuge with his family in Grand Canyon. In 1867 his people surrendered to the military and made the Long Walk into captivity at Fort Sumner, New Mexico. When allowed to return home, Etsidi became a headman who worked to protect his people and preserve their lands. He traveled to Washington, D.C., and met with Teddy Roosevelt, who extended the reservation to include many of the Navajo living along the Little Colorado. But unknown to Etsidi, his own lands had been ceded to the railroad. He was forced across the river into more barren country, retaining a small inholding within the national monument.

Reaching the highway, Dave and I cross the river and leave the desert. We have one last stop to make before heading home. Pulling off the road at Cameron, we look up James Peshlakai, the grandson of Peshlakai Etsidi. James served as chapter president for sixteen years, where he gained a reputation as an outspoken defender of his people. Not having had a chance to call ahead, we take our chances. Dave knocks on the front door, and we hear a voice inside directing us to the rear of the house. James stands in the doorway to greet us, his face painted red with hematite. He has a blue bandana tied in a broad headband and is wearing moccasins. Troubled by the death of old friends, he tells us he's been up all night undergoing an Enemyway ceremony.

We take seats in the living room, and I notice furniture barricading the front door. This doesn't make sense until I realize the back door points east, the direction a traditional hogan faces. This orientation opens the home to the presence of the Holy People and the blessings of life. Grounded in an oral tradition, James begins telling us stories, working in history, politics, and tradition. He expresses his opinions bluntly, taking an assertive approach I suspect he learned in his dealings with various government entities. When James tells us he was forced off his family's land at Wupatki, I mention the old Navajo sites in the area dating back to the 1820s. He stops me.

"We've been here since the Third World," he says, and proceeds to state his case by going back to the origin of things. After working up to the Fifth World, the one we now inhabit, he adds, "My grandfather told me those worlds really existed. He told me, 'You can see for yourself. Go to the bottom of the Grand Canyon and look at the rock—unformed, dark. That's the First World. Then came the Second World—turquoise and the first insects.' You can find those trilobites there. And now we live in the Glittering World. Look around!"

Hearing about our trip, James wants to head back with us. His family has a place out there, and he likes that country. He comes up with an idea. Years ago he found an unusual rock formation when he was crossing the desert on foot and will show it to us. "It's shaped like a cow!" he says. "It's red and even has the white spots. It's kicking up its feet. You've got to see it!"

Caught up in his enthusiasm, the three of us are back in the trucks and recrossing the bridge before we know it. Some people go to the desert for solitude, others for beauty, and some simply to escape. We're returning to the Painted Desert to search for a cow-shaped rock. For some of us that's reason enough.

# further reading

Sidney Ash, *Petrified Forest: A Story in Stone*. Petrified Forest, Ariz.: Petrified Forest
    Museum Association, 2005.

Roland T. Bird, *Bones for Barnum Brown: Adventures of a Dinosaur Hunter*. Fort
    Worth: Texas Christian University Press, 1985.

Janice Bowers, *Seasons of the Wind: A Naturalist's Look at the Plant Life of Southwestern
    Sand Dunes*. Flagstaff, Ariz.: Northland Press, 1986.

Rose Houk, *The Painted Desert: Land of Light and Shadow*. Petrified Forest, Ariz.:
    Petrified Forest Museum Association, 1990.

A. Trinkle Jones, *Stalking the Past: Prehistory at the Petrified Forest.* Petrified Forest, Ariz.: Petrified Forest Museum Association, 1993.

Robert A. Long and Rose Houk, *Dawn of the Dinosaurs: The Triassic in the Petrified Forest.* Petrified Forest, Ariz.: Petrified Forest Museum Association, 1988.

George M. Lubick, *Petrified Forest National Park: A Wilderness Bound in Time.* Tucson: University of Arizona Press, 1996.

# travel in the painted desert

Petrified Forest National Park, east of Holbrook, Arizona, offers the best introduction to the Painted Desert. While the entire park lies within the desert, visitors can stop at viewpoints north of Interstate 40 and the overlooks at Blue Mesa for expansive views of colorful badlands. For those wanting to leave their vehicle behind, day hikes and overnight backpacking trips can be made into the park's Painted Desert wilderness areas. Contact the Petrified Forest National Park headquarters in Arizona for further information.

Outside the park, two highways pass through fine sections of the desert. Highway 87 north of Winslow skirts an impressive badlands at the Little Painted

Desert County Park. Highway 89 north of Cameron crosses miles of classic desert landscape, best viewed early or late in the day for the most dramatic colors.

On the Navajo reservation, visitors traveling on unpaved roads, camping, or hiking need permits. They can be obtained by contacting the Navajo Nation Parks and Recreation Department in Window Rock, Arizona. Visitors must comply with tribal regulations and respect the privacy of the Navajo people. Even with a tribal permit, it is customary to introduce yourself to the local families and let them know your intentions.

Fossils, petrified wood, and human artifacts found on federal, state, and tribal lands cannot be collected without scientific permits. Laws, including the Paleontological Resource Protection Act of 2003, protect these unique resources and enable us to pass on this heritage to future generations.

## about the author

Scott Thybony is an anthropologist by education and a writer by profession. He has written books and articles for National Geographic, and his work has appeared in major newspapers and magazines. *Burntwater,* published by the University of Arizona Press, was chosen as a finalist for a PEN literary award in creative nonfiction. The Flagstaff resident has lived with native peoples in the American Southwest and the Arctic, and the subjects of his interviews have ranged from medicine men to astronauts. His extensive travels have resulted in award-winning articles for magazines such as *Smithsonian, Men's Journal,* and *Outside.* The former river guide and archeologist brings to his writing an enthusiasm for remote places and the people who inhabit them.

## about the photographer

Freelance photographer David Edwards has been documenting the wilds of the Southwest, as well as remote regions in Africa, South America, and Asia for more than sixteen years. He has made more than a dozen trips to Mongolia. His photographic essay of the Kazakh Eagle Hunters in western Mongolia appeared in *National Geographic* magazine in 1999, and his striking images have been published in numerous national and international publications. Recently, his work appeared in *National Geographic's 100 Best Photographs,* in a special collector's edition, volume 1. David Edwards now lives and works in Flagstaff, Arizona.

Library of Congress Cataloging-in-Publication Data
Thybony, Scott.
The Painted Desert : land of wind and stone / text by Scott Thybony ;
photographs by David Edwards.
p. cm. – (Desert places)
Includes bibliographical references.
ISBN-13: 978-0-8165-2480-8 (pbk. : alk. paper)
ISBN-10: 0-8165-2480-7 (pbk. : alk. paper)
1. Painted Desert (Ariz.)  2. Thybony, Scott—Travel—
Arizona—Painted Desert.  I. Title.  II. Series.
F817.P2T47 2006
979.1'33–dc22
                                              2006006377